BOSTON
TO
LINCOLN

Also lines from Louth and Horncastle

Vic Mitchell and Keith Smith

MP Middleton Press

Front cover: The north end of Lincoln station is seen on 17th March 1993, as no. 156403 leaves for Coventry at 11.54. A class 08 diesel awaits further shunting work. (M.J.Stretton)

Back cover: The complexity of ownership in the Lincoln area is shown on the Railway Clearing House map of 1897.

Published 26 September 2015
First reprint January 2017

ISBN 978 1 908174 80 2

© Middleton Press, 2015

Design Deborah Esher
Typesetting Catherine Nayler

Published by
          Middleton Press
          Easebourne Lane
          Midhurst
          West Sussex
          GU29 9AZ
Tel: 01730 813169
Fax: 01730 812601
Email: info@middletonpress.co.uk
www.middletonpress.co.uk

Printed and bound by CPI Group (UK) Ltd, Croydon, CR0 4YY

INDEX

CONTENTS

. The Railway Clearing House
map for 1947.

ACKNOWLEDGEMENTS

We are very grateful for the assistance received from many of those mentioned in the credits, also to M.Back, C.L.Caddy, A.J.Castledine, G.Croughton, M.Dart, G.Gartside, S.C.Jenkins, N.Langridge, B.Lewis, J.P.McCrickard, A.C.Mott, Mr D. and Dr. S.Salter, A.Stennett, T.Walsh and in particular our always supportive wives, Barbara Mitchell and Janet Smith.

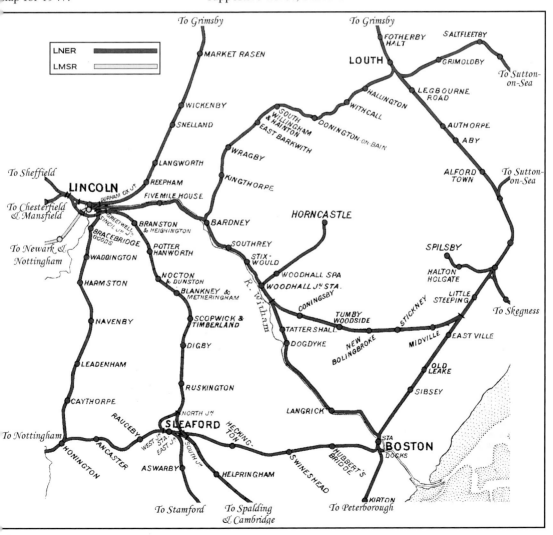

GEOGRAPHICAL SETTING

The entire route of the main line in this album was built close to the River Witham. Its valley had once formed a long narrow bay on the North Sea coast, running inland from Boston to Lincoln. Reclaimed largely by Dutch engineers, the southern part is still known as Holland Fen. The ground gradually sank, but became rich fertile agricultural land.

The high ground east of the Witham Valley is known as the Wolds, comprising chalk hills and areas of sandstone and clay; Lough stands on the chalk. All the lines were built in Lincolnshire and the higher parts of its flat areas were to prove to be of value for the airfields in the World Wars.

Rising north of Donington-on-Bain is the River Bain, which flowed under the line there and ran south to pass close to the northern mile of the Horncastle branch. It continued south to join the River Witham, close to Dogdyke station.

The maps are to the scale of 25ins to 1 mile, with north at the top, unless otherwise indicated. The historical quotations are from Bradshaw's Guide of 1866.

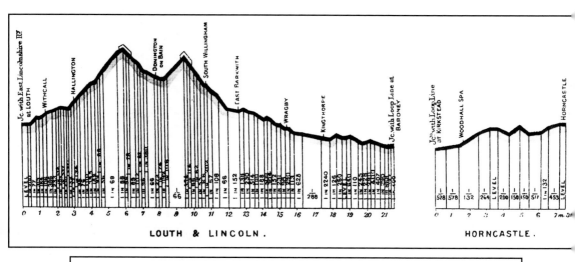

LOUTH & LINCOLN.   HORNCASTLE.

March

HISTORICAL BACKGROUND

Boston received lines from the north and the south in 1848, the line northwest to Lincoln opening on 17th October of that year. This line and the one from Spalding were opened by the Great Northern Railway. The former was known as the Lincolnshire Loop Line and is featured herein.

Lincoln had the Midland Railway arrive from Newark in 1846, followed by the GNR as above, plus its link to Gainsborough in 1849. A GNR line from the north, through Market Rasen, came in 1848. One from the west opened in 1896, this becoming part of the Great Central Railway in 1907. The GNR operated the branch to Horncastle, which came into use on 11th August 1855. It was owned by a separate company until 1923.

The GNR opened the route from Bardney to Louth in stages: for goods to South Willingham on 9th November 1874, to Donington-on-Bain by 27th September 1875 and to Louth on 26th June 1876. Passengers were carried throughout from 1st December 1876.

The GNR became a constituent of the London & North Eastern Railway in 1923, most of which became the Eastern Region of British Railways upon nationalisation in 1948.

Passenger traffic to Horncastle ended on 13th September 1954 and between Bardney and Louth on 5th November 1951. However, it ceased on both lines between 11th September 1939 and 4th December 1939 for wartime reasons. Freight withdrawals are detailed in the captions.

The Boston to Lincoln service was terminated on 17th June 1963, but Bardney northwards continued to receive trains from Firsby to Lincoln until 5th October 1970. The service from Boston to Peterborough also ceased that day.

July 1878

PASSENGER SERVICES

The tables below indicate the number of down trains stopping at most stations, on at least five days per week. The timetable extracts give an indication of the destinations of the few faster long distance trains, as do the captions.

Boston to Lincoln

	Weekdays	Sundays
1850	4	1
1882	5	1
1912	6	1
1942	4	1
1962	7	1

Louth to Bardney

	Weekdays	Sundays
1878	4	0
1907	4	0
1937	5	0
1950	3	0

Horncastle Branch

	Weekdays	Sundays
1855	5	0
1877	4	0
1895	5	0
1925	8	0
1951	5	0

The Horncastle branch had some trains on Sundays until 1868.

July 1913

September 1925

PETERBRO', SPALDING, BOSTON, BARDNEY, and LINCOLN.—L. & N. E.

Miles	Down.	Week Days. aft	mrn	mrn b	mrn	mrn F	mrn W	mrn G	mrn	mrn	aft b	mrn		aft S	aft d	aft	aft		aft	aft b	aft		Suns. non	
	688 London (King's Cross) dep.	1045	4 45	....	5 5	....	7A15	7A15	....	S 45	....	1130	....	1A40	....	3 0	4A0	Through Train, London (King's Cross) to Grimsby Town (arr. 7 54 aft.) and Cleethorpes (arr. 8 17 aft.), see pages 734 and 820; also Through Carriage from London (King's Cross) to Horncastle (arr. 7 32 aft.), see page 733.	....	....	5A45	....	12A0	....
—	Peterbro' (North) dep.	3 10	6 45	....	7 40	....	9 30	9 30	....	1050	....	2 10	....	3 22	....	4 40	5 50		....	....	7 18	....	2 5	....
5½	Peakirk A	mrn	6 55	....	7 51	....	....	9 41	....	11 0	....	2 21	....	3 33	....	4 50	....		....	....	7 29	....	2 15	....
7	Deeping St. James B	....	6 59	....	7 55	....	9 42	9 46	....	11 4	....	2 25	....	3 37	....	4 55	....		....	....	7 34	....	2 19	....
11½	Littleworth	....	7 8	....	8 3	....	....	9 54	....	1112	....	2 33	....	3 46	....	5 3	....		....	....	7 42	....	2 27	....
16½	Spalding 754, 942 arr.	3 33	7 16	....	8 11	....	9 55	10 3	....	1120	....	2 42	....	3 54	....	5 11	6 12		....	....	7 51	....	2 34	....
	Spalding dep.	3 38	7 18	....	8 15	....	9 57	....	....	1130	....	2 47	....	4 10	....	5 21	6 15		....	....	7 53	....	2 36	....
20¾	Surfleet	....	7 26	....	8 23	....	10 5	....	....	1138	....	2 56	....	4 18	....	5 29	....		....	....	8 2	....	2 44	....
24¼	Algarkirk and Sutterton	....	7 32	....	8 29	....	1011	....	....	1145	....	3 3	....	4 25	....	5 35	....		....	....	8 9	....	2 50	....
27	Kirton	....	7 38	....	8 35	....	1017	....	....	1151	....	3 9	....	4 31	....	5 41	....		....	....	8 15	....	2 56	....
31	Boston 734, 736 arr.	3 58	7 46	....	8 43	....	1025	....	....	1159	....	3 17	....	4 39	....	5 49	6 33		....	....	8 23	....	3 4	....
	Boston dep.	....	7 52	....	....	9 40	....	....	1050	1220	....	3 34	....	....	....	5 58	....		6 45	....	....	....	3 11	....
35½	Langrick	....	8 1	....	....	9 49	....	....	....	1229	....	3 43	....	....	....	6 7	....		....	....	....	....	3 20	....
42	Dogdyke	....	8 11	....	....	9 59	....	....	....	1239	....	3 53	....	....	....	6 17	....		....	....	....	....	3 30	....
42¾	Tattershall	....	8 15	....	....	10 3	....	....	11 8	1243	....	3 57	....	....	....	6 21	....		....	....	....	....	3 34	....
46½	Woodhall Junction 733 arr.	....	8 22	....	....	1010	....	....	1114	1250	....	4 5	....	....	....	6 28	....		7 7	....	....	....	3 42	....
—	735 Skegness dep.	....	6 35	7 55	....	....	....	....	....	....	1250	....	....	....	3 20	....	....		....	6 35	....	....	....	....
—	733 Firsby "	....	7 25	8 40	....	....	....	....	....	....	1 25	....	....	....	4 20	....	....		....	6 58	....	....	....	....
—	Woodhall Junction dep.	....	8 25	9 30	....	1012	....	....	1116	1253	2 3	4 8	....	....	5 6	6 32	....		....	7 43	....	....	3 43	....
48½	Stixwould	....	8 30	....	....	1017	....	....	....	1258	....	4 13	....	....	....	6 37	....		....	....	....	....	3 48	....
50¼	Southrey	....	8 35	....	....	1023	....	....	....	1 3	....	4 18	....	....	....	6 42	....		....	....	....	....	3 53	....
52¾	Bardney 737 arr.	....	8 40	9 41	....	1028	....	....	1123	1 8	2 11	4 23	....	....	5 16	6 47	....		....	7 53	....	....	3 58	....
	Bardney dep.	....	8 43	9 43	....	1030	....	....	1127	1 9	2 12	4 27	....	....	5 17	6 48	....		....	7 54	....	....	3 59	....
56¾	Five Mile House	....	8 51	....	....	1038	....	....	....	1 17	....	4 35	....	....	....	6 56	....		....	....	....	....	4 7	....
59¼	Washingboro' [822, 823	....	8 57	9 53	....	....	....	....	....	1 23	2 22	4 41	....	....	....	7 2	....		....	....	....	....	4 13	....
62	Lincoln 600, 755, 814 arr.	....	9 8	10 3	....	1050	....	....	1145	1 33	2 32	4 50	....	....	5 34	7 13	....		....	8 13	....	....	4 21	....

Miles	Up.	Week Days. mrn	mrn	mrn	mrn b	mrn		mrn	mrn d		aft	aft	aft G	aft W	aft F	aft	aft b	aft b	aft	aft	aft	aft	Suns. mrn	aft
	Lincoln (L. N. E.) dep.	....	7 55	....	9 15	....	Through Train, Cleethorpes (dep. 8 53 mrn.) and Grimsby Town (dep. 9 15 mrn.), to London (King's Cross), see pages 821 and 735; also Through Carriage from Horncastle (dep. 9 10 mrn.) to London (King's Cross), see page 733.	1033	1120	....	1240	....	....	....	3 5	3 52	4 10	6 10	....	....	6 30	....	....	5 53
2½	Washingboro'	....	8 1	....	....	....		1040	....	....	....	....	....	....	....	....	4 16	6 16	....	....	6 36	....	....	5 59
5¼	Five Mile House	....	8 6	....	....	....		1046	....	....	....	....	....	....	....	....	4 21	....	....	....	6 41	....	....	6 4
9¼	Bardney arr.	....	8 14	....	9 29	....		1054	....	....	....	....	....	....	3 20	4 7	4 29	6 26	....	....	6 49	....	....	6 12
	Bardney dep.	....	8 15	....	9 30	....		1057	....	....	....	....	....	....	3 22	4 11	4 33	6 27	....	....	6 52	....	....	6 14
11¾	Southrey	....	8 20	....	....	....		11 2	....	....	....	....	....	....	3 27	4 16	....	....	....	....	6 57	....	....	6 19
13¼	Stixwould	....	8 25	....	....	....		11 7	....	....	....	....	....	....	3 32	4 21	....	....	....	....	7 2	....	....	6 24
15¾	Woodhall Junction 733 arr.	....	8 30	....	9 39	....		1112	1143	....	1 3	....	....	....	3 37	4 26	4 43	6 37	....	....	7 7	....	....	6 29
35¼	733 Firsby arr.	....	9 23	....	1013	....		....	1228	....	....	....	....	....	....	....	5 29	7 21	....	....	....	....	....	....
45	734 Skegness "	....	....	....	1038	....		....	1 55	....	....	....	....	....	....	....	6 0	7 59	....	....	....	....	....	....
—	Woodhall Junction dep.	....	8 35	....	....	9 45		1115	....	....	1 5	....	....	....	3 40	4 31	....	....	....	....	7 11	....	....	6 31
19¾	Tattershall	....	8 42	....	....	9 52		1122	....	....	....	....	....	....	3 48	4 38	....	....	....	....	7 18	....	....	6 38
20	Dogdyke	....	8 46	....	....	9 56		1126	....	....	....	....	....	....	3 52	4 42	....	....	....	....	7 21	....	....	6 42
26¼	Langrick	....	8 56	....	....	10 6		1135	....	....	....	....	....	....	4 2	4 52	....	....	....	....	7 30	....	....	6 52
31	Boston 734, 736 arr.	....	9 5	....	....	1016		1145	....	....	1 27	....	....	....	4 12	5 2	....	....	....	....	7 39	....	....	7 2
	Boston dep.	7 37	....	9 50	....	1036		1152	....	....	....	1 45	....	2 28	....	5 12	....	....	6 55	7 15	....	9 37	1150	7 10
35	Kirton	7 45	....	9 58	....	....		12 0	....	....	....	1 53	....	2 36	....	5 20	....	....	....	7 23	....	u	1158	7 18
37¾	Algarkirk and Sutterton	7 51	....	10 4	....	....		12 6	....	....	....	....	....	2 42	....	5 26	....	....	....	7 29	....	....	12 4	7 24
41¼	Surfleet	7 58	....	1011	....	....		1213	....	....	....	....	....	2 49	....	5 35	....	....	....	7 36	....	....	1211	7 31
45½	Spalding 755, 943 arr.	8 5	....	1018	....	1054		1220	....	....	....	2 7	....	2 56	....	5 42	....	....	7 13	7 44	....	9 58	1218	7 38
	Spalding dep.	8 11	....	1025	....	1058		1225	....	....	....	2 11	2 43	2 59	....	5 48	....	....	7 18	7 50	....	10 1	1221	7 41
50½	Littleworth	8 20	....	1034	....	....		1234	....	....	....	....	2 52	3 8	....	5 57	....	....	....	7 59	....	a	....	7 50
55	Deeping St. James B	8 28	....	1042	....	....		1242	....	....	....	....	3 0	3 16	....	6 5	....	....	....	8 7	....	....	....	7 58
56¾	Peakirk A [695, 759	8 32	....	1047	....	....		1247	....	....	....	....	3 4	3 21	....	6 9	....	....	....	8 12	....	....	....	8 3
62	Peterbro (North) 688, arr.	8 47	....	1058	....	1122		1 0	....	....	....	2 33	3 14	3 31	....	6 20	....	....	7 45	8 23	....	1023	1250	8 15
138¾	695 London (King's Cross) arr.	1040	....	....	....	1 5		3 50	....	....	....	4A30	5A10	5A10	....	8 50	....	....	9A25	....	....	3 35	3A45	10A20

NOTES.

- **A** Station for Crowland (5½ miles).
- **A** Restaurant Cars between King's Cross and Peterbro'.
- **a** Stops on Saturdays to set down.
- **B** Station for Market Deeping (3¼ miles) and Crowland (4½ miles).
- **b** Through Trains between Skegness and Lincoln.
- **C** L. N. E.
- **d** Through Trains between Firsby and Lincoln.
- **F** Fridays only.
- **G** Tuesdays only.
- **S** Saturdays only.
- **u** Stops to set down and on Saturdays at 9 45 aft. to take up or set down.
- **W** Wednesdays only.

September 1925

LOUTH and BARDNEY.

Miles	Up.	Week Days only. mrn	mrn		aft	aft	aft	
	Louth dep.	7 45	9 56	..	1215	3 10	5 52	..
3	Hallington	..	10 2	..	..	3 16	5 58	..
4¾	Withcall	7 54	10 7	..	..	3 21	6 3	..
7¾	Donington-on-Bain	8 3	1016	..	1231	3 30	6 12	..
10¾	South Willingham and	8 10	1023	..	Bb	3 37	6 19	..
12¾	East Barkwith [Hainton	8 14	1027	..	Bb	3 41	6 23	..
15½	Wragby	8 20	1033	..	1246	3 47	6 29	..
17½	Kingthorpe	8 24	1037	..	..	3 51	6 33	..
21½	Bardney 887 arr.	8 31	1044	..	1257	3 58	6 40	..
30¾	887 Lincoln (L.N.E.) arr.	9 7	11 4	..	1 22	4 41	7 7	..
160¾	887 London (K. C.) "	..	3 47	..	4 20	9 13	..	..

Miles	Down.	Week Days only. mrn		mrn		mrn		mrn		aft	
	887 London (K. C.) dep.	4 45	..	7b25	..	8 45	..	11 30	..	3 0	..
	887 Lincoln (L.N.E.) "	8 25	..	1038	..	12 44	..	4 12	..	6 30	..
—	Bardney dep.	8 45	..	1129	..	1 18	..	4 32	..	6 55	..
4	Kingthorpe	8 52	..	..	..	1 25	..	4 39	..	7 2	..
6	Wragby	8 58	..	1139	..	1 31	..	4 45	..	7 8	..
8¾	East Barkwith ..[Hainton	9 3	..	1144	..	1 36	..	4 50	..	7 13	..
10¾	South Willingham and	9 8	..	1149	..	1 41	..	4 55	..	7 18	..
13¾	Donington-on-Bain	9 15	..	1157	..	1 49	..	5 2	..	7 25	..
16¾	Withcall	9 21	..	12 3	..	1 55	..	5 8	..	7 31	..
18½	Hallington	9 25	..	12 7	..	1 59	..	5 12	..	..	..
21½	Louth 888, 890 arr.	9 31	..	1213	..	2 5	..	5 18	..	7 40	..

June 1937

June 1950

Table 73 — **LOUTH and BARDNEY**

Miles		Week Days only a.m		p.m		p.m		
	Louth dep	7 48		1240	..	3 57	..	
3	Hallington	..	..	1246	..	Aa	..	..
4¾	Withcall	7 59	..	1251	..	4 8	..	..
7¾	Donington-on-Bain	8 7	..	1 0	..	4 17	..	..
10¾	South Willingham and	8 14	..	1 7	..	4 24	..	..
12½	EastBarkwith ...[Hainton	8 18	..	1 11	..	4 28	..	..
15½	Wragby	8 24	..	1 18	..	4 34	..	..
17½	Kingthorpe	8 28	..	1 22	..	4 38	..	..
21½	Bardney arr	8 36	..	1 29	..	4 46	..	..
30¾	65 Lincoln arr	9 3	..	2 1	..	5 36	..	..
150½	65 London (King's C.) "	1 20	..	5B19	..	9D46	..	..

Miles		Week Days only a.m		a.m		p.m	
	65 London (King's C.) .. dep	4 0	..	8K10	..	1L20	..
	65 Lincoln "	9 20	..	1 20	..	6 0	..
—	Bardney dep	9 55	..	1 50	..	6 25	..
4	Kingthorpe	10 2	..	1 57	..	6 32	..
6	Wragby	10 8	..	2 3	..	6 38	..
9	East Barkwith ..[Hainton	1013	..	2 8	..	6 43	..
10¾	South Willingham and	1018	..	2 13	..	6 48	..
13¾	Donington-on-Bain	1025	..	2 21	..	6 55	..
16¾	Withcall	1031	..	2 27	..	7 1	..
18½	Hallington	Aa	..	2 31	..	..	..
21½	Louth arr	1041	..	2 37	..	7 21	..

Aa Stops when required — B Via Lincoln — D Via Lincoln. Arr. 9 37 on Fridays and 9 50 p.m. on Saturdays

K Via Lincoln. On Saturdays dep. 8 5 a.m., via Boston, (6 55 a.m. on 23rd September via Lincoln)

L Via Lincoln. Dep. 1 35 p.m. on Saturdays

1. Boston to Lincoln
BOSTON

II. The 1905 edition at 6ins to 1 mile shows our route at the top left corner and the Grimsby line diverging to the right from it. The Spalding route is at the bottom, while the Sleaford line joins it from the left, at Sleaford Junction. The Haven is lower right and provides the link to the North Sea. Broadfield Lane (lower left) runs close to the northern boundary of the engine shed area and then crosses the main lines; eight tracks in total, on the level.

Skirbeck Quarter

1.   Two through lines were provided and the splendid platform canopies were completed in 1850. More waiting rooms were added in 1911. Road transport awaits on the right. (P.Laming coll.)

2.   Class D3 4-4-0 no.4311 was ex-GNR and was photographed on 18th June 1933. The loco shed and workshops were south of the station and British Rail coded them 40F. There was a 55ft turntable, but depot closure came in January 1964. (H.F.Wheeler/R.S.Carpenter)

3.   In the background is the footbridge, which had its roof finished in 1864. This view south is from 1954 and includes fine brick arching. (Stations UK)

4.   Class 4MT 2-6-0 no. 43059 is working a special tour with the District Engineers Inspection Saloon on 16th February 1954. It also served as a meeting room at various locations. (P.J.Kelley)

5.   A 1964 northward view has a train in the up platform and the barrow crossing in front of it. The barrow crossing needed careful use. (Stations UK)

6.	This 1969 view in the other direction was recorded from the footbridge. West Street Junction Box was built in 1874 and became a listed building. Its 60 levers were reduced to 36 in 1974, but the box was still in use in 2015. (Milepost 92½)

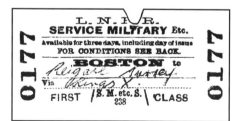

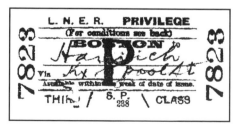

7.   This is a northward panorama from 1969 and includes the staff crossing. The main lines were taken out of use on 19th May 1974. In the distance is Grand Sluice signal box and the gas holder. (Milepost 92½)

8.   Two photographs from March 1992 complete our survey. The lattice bridge was replaced by one without supports, but the new canopies did have them. The platforms could take eight coaches each. (A.C.Hartless)

9.   This is the east façade and the nearest part was added in 1911. The car park area on the right in the distance was originally the site of carriage sidings. The goods depot was south of the station. There were also five private sidings. (A.C.Hartless)

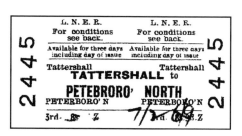

10.   The first bridge over the River Witham had been of timber construction and this later one was completed in 1885. Nearby was Grand Sluice Box, which had a 36-lever frame and was in use from 1891 to 1985. It took over the work of East Lincoln Junction Box on 18th May 1924. (P.Laming coll.)

Other views of Boston station appear in *Spalding to Grimsby* **and** *Nottingham to Boston*. **The former also features Boston Docks.**

LANGRICK

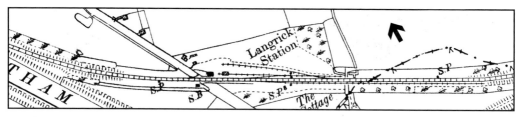

III. The 1913 survey includes both sidings and is at about 9ins to 1 mile. Hall Hills Regional Sleeper Depot was developed in this area. Also present was a pumping station for locomotive and station water supply.

11.   Seen in 1961 is the unusual bell tower, which differed from the towers on the stations further north. The goods shed is in the background; freight traffic ceased on the same day as passenger service, in 1963. (Stations UK)

12.   A 1963 view gives a glimpse through the tower and of part of the signal box, near the left seat. It opened in 1876 and had 25 levers. Its neighbours to the south were Halls Hill (25 levers) and Antons Gowt (5 levers); the latter closed in 1902. (Stations UK)

13.   The signalman's view is also from 1963 and it includes the tie rod for bracing the very long gate. He could enjoy the pantiles on the belfry. In its later years, the box was usually manned 24 hours per day. (Stations UK)

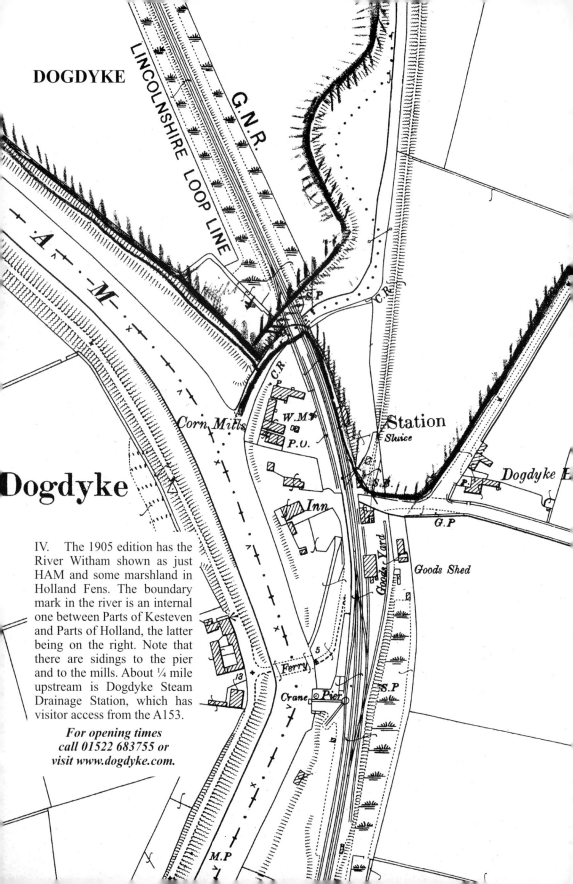

DOGDYKE

LINCOLNSHIRE LOOP LINE

G.N.R.

Corn Mills

Dogdyke

W.M*

P.O.

Station

Sluice

Inn

Dogdyke E

G.P

Goods Shed

Goods Yard

IV.   The 1905 edition has the
River Witham shown as just
HAM and some marshland in
Holland Fens. The boundary
mark in the river is an internal
one between Parts of Kesteven
and Parts of Holland, the latter
being on the right. Note that
there are sidings to the pier
and to the mills. About ¼ mile
upstream is Dogdyke Steam
Drainage Station, which has
visitor access from the A153.

*For opening times
call 01522 683755 or
visit www.dogdyke.com.*

Ferry

5

13

Crane

Pier

S.P

M.P

14.   The station was two miles west of New York and had Italianate styling, the tower being formed by two fenestrated chimney stacks. The goods shed is visible beyond the station house in this postcard view. The house was still in use in 2015. (A.J.Ludlam coll.)

15.   The River Witham was made navigable from the sea to Lincoln and canals were built from Dogdyke north to Horncastle and southwest to Sleaford. There were several local ferries; three are shown here. Nearest is a punt, next is the chain ferry and beyond it is a boat for groups of people. All the main station buildings are on the right. (A.J.Ludlam coll.)

16.   The small number of staff pose for a postcard producer. There would be limited sales, as the local population amounted to 180 folk in 1901. The signal box was built in 1878 and had 30 levers. (P.Laming coll.)

17.   A 1953 northward view reveals well-kept gardens; the staff had adequate spare time in that era, as there were only six trains stopping each way on weekdays, with one on Sundays. Above the ballast wagons is the roof of the former mill. The wagons are standing in the former private siding. (Stations UK)

18.   It is 21st October 1961 and class B1 4-6-0 no. 61282 is working the 3.51pm from Boston to Doncaster. Anglers formed a substantial portion of the passenger traffic at the rural stations on the route. (D.K.Jones coll.)

19.   The neglected shrubbery is seen from the front of the last direct train from Lincoln to Boston. The date is 16th June 1963. The goods shed had been provided with a one-ton crane. Oil lamps continued to the end. (B.I.Nathan)

TATTERSHALL

V. The 1947 edition is scaled at about 5ins to 1 mile.

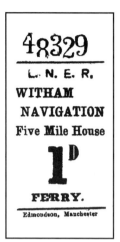

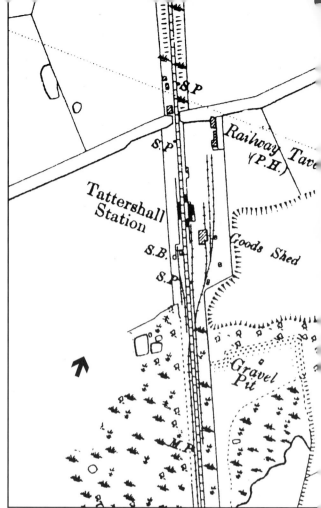

20. Bound for Boston is Stirling 2-2-2 no. 4, which was completed in 1868. It has just passed over the foot crossing. The goods yard seems busy, but the date is unknown. The population was 474 in 1901 and 828 in 1961.
(R.M.Casserley coll.)

21.   A southward view in about 1963 includes the busy coal merchant and a van by the goods shed, which was fitted with a 25cwt. crane. The pole on the left carries stay wires for the perforated concrete signal post on the right. (Stations UK)

22.   A northward panorama in 1962 has part of the goods yard on the right. It would close on 17th June 1963 and all services would cease. About ½ mile to the east was the village centre, with its fine castle remains. The 1876 signal box had 25 levers and closed with the line. (E. Wilmshurst)

23.   Yellow brickwork was used on all but one station on the route. DMUs were introduced on the loop line in 1959 and this one is running to Lincoln on 10th November 1962. Fifty years later, the buildings were in use as a dwelling and art studio. (E.Wilmshurst)

TATTERSHALL.

Telegraph station at Kirkstead, 3½ miles.
MARKET DAY.—Tuesday.
FAIRS.—Friday after May 4, and 14, Sept. 25.
MONEY ORDER OFFICE at Coningsby, 5½ miles
In its ruined yet beautiful church is a brass to Sir R. Cromwell, the ruins of whose castle (built in 1440) is close at hand, with its well preserved keep, 100 feet high. In the vicinity are *Scrivelsby*, seat of the hereditary champion of England, Sir H. Dymoke, whose family tomb is at Horncastle, so famous for its August horse fair ; *Hooseholme Priory*, Earl of Winchelsea, and Sleaford, with its spire church and handsome cross.

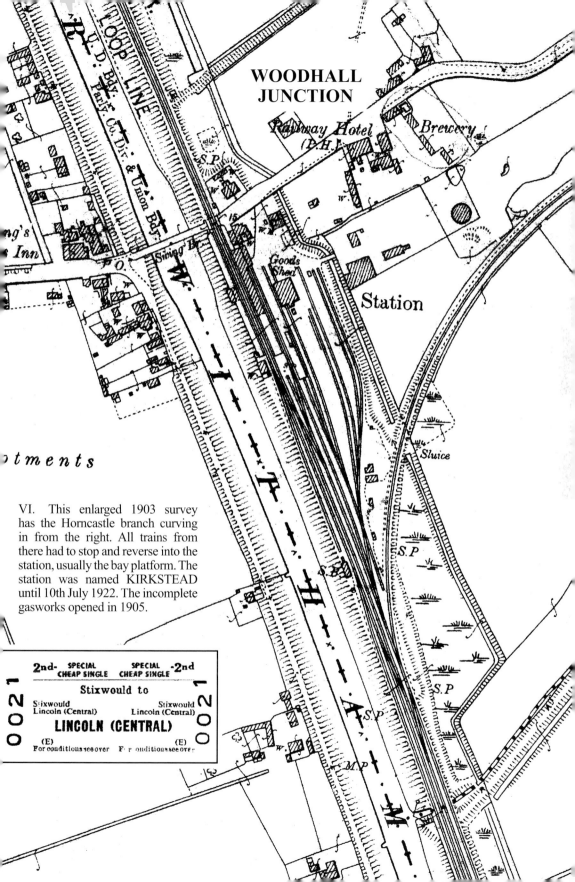

WOODHALL JUNCTION

Railway Hotel (P.H.)

Brewery

R.U.D. Bdy. Park Co. Dis. & Union Bdy.

LOOP LINE

S.P

ng's Inn

Swing B'

Goods Shed

Station

otments

Sluice

S.P

VI. This enlarged 1903 survey has the Horncastle branch curving in from the right. All trains from there had to stop and reverse into the station, usually the bay platform. The station was named KIRKSTEAD until 10th July 1922. The incomplete gasworks opened in 1905.

S.P

S.P

S.P

M.P

2nd-	SPECIAL CHEAP SINGLE	SPECIAL CHEAP SINGLE	-2nd

Stixwould to

Stixwould
Lincoln (Central)

Stixwould
Lincoln (Central)

LINCOLN (CENTRAL)

(E)

(E)

For conditions see over   For conditions see over

0021   0021

24. This fascinating picture dates from prior to 1889, when the swing bridge was completed. The roofs of all the main buildings are included. The goods shed (right) housed a 25cwt. crane. (Stations UK)

February 1942

Table 52 PETERBOROUGH (North), SPALDING, BOSTON, and LINCOLN (via Boston)

Miles		Week Days aft	mn	mn	mrn	mrn	mrn	aft	mrn	aft	aft	aft S	aft V	aft	aft	Sun. mrn	aft	aft
	1 London (King'sC.) dep	11F15		430	..	..	7 25		10R10	1R15	..	3 5	4 5	..	5R50	11R10	..	510
—	Peterboro' (North). dep	2 40	..	645	..	..	1054	..	1 23	3 0		5 7	5 50	To Horncastle arr. 7 39 aft. (Table 53)	7 50	1 35	..	731
5½	Peakirk	mrn	..	656	..	..	11 5	..	1 34	..	TC Skegness to Lincoln	5 21	..		8 1	aft	..	..
7	St. James Deeping B	..	..	7 0	..	..	11 9	..	1 38	..		5 25	..		8 5	..	..	..
11½	Littleworth	..	..	7 8	..	..	1117	..	1 46	..		5 33	..		8 13	..	..	..
16½	Spalding arr	3 5	..	717	..	..	1126	..	1 55	3 23		5 42	6 14		8 22	2 0	..	755
	Spalding dep	3 15	..	721		..	1134	..	1 59	3 28		5 46	6 18		8 30	2 5	..	759
20½	Surfleet	..	..	729	TC Skegness to Lincoln	..	1142	..	2 7	..		5 54	..		8 38	2 13	..	..
24½	Algarkirk & Sutterton	..	.	736		..	1149	..	2 14	..		6 1	..		8 45	2 20	..	..
27	Kirton	..	..	742		..	1155	..	2 20	..		6 7	..		8 51	2 26	..	..
31	Boston arr	3 34	..	750		..	12 3	..	2 28	3 48		6 15	6 39		8 59	2 34	..	820
	Boston dep	..	625	755		1110		1 40	..	4 10			..	6 50	..	..	2 46	..
35¾	Langrick	..	..	8 4		1119	Stop	1 49	..	4 19			..	6 59	..	..	2 55	..
42	Dogdyke	..	Aa	814		1129	..	1 59	..	4 29			..	7 9	..	..	3 5	..
42¾	Tattershall	..	Aa	817		1132	aft	2 2	..	4 32			..	7 12	..	..	3 11	..
46½	Woodhall Junction..arr	..	654	824		1139	T	2 9	..	4 39			..	7 19	..	..	3 18	..
—	59 Skegness dep	..	..	..	8 0	..	1220	..	..	..	4 0	TC and Buffet Car, King's Cross to Boston	..	..	..	..	..	..
—	59 Firsby "	..	..	..	8 40	..	1255	..	..	..	445		..	..	..	..	..	..
—	Woodhall Junction. dep	..	..	827	9 30	1141	1 36	2 11	..	4 41	528		..	..	..	..	3 23	..
48½	Stixwould	..	..	..	9 35	..	..	2 16	..	4 46	..		..	..	..	..	3 28	..
50¼	Southrey	..	..	834	9 40	..	..	2 21	..	4.51	..		..	..	..	..	3 33	..
52¾	Bardney arr	..	..	839	9 45	1151	1 47	2 26	..	4 56	539		..	..	..	..	3 38	..
	Bardney dep	..	..	841	9 47	1153	1 48	2 28	..	4 58	541		..	..	..	..	3 41	..
56¾	Five Mile House	..	..	..	9 55	..	..	2 36	..	..	..		..	..	..	..	3 49	..
59½	Washingborough ¶	..	..	..	..	..	..	..	..	..	..		..	..	..	..	..	..
62	Lincoln arr	..	..	856	10 4	12 8	2 3	2 45	..	5 13	558		..	..	..	..	3 59	..

Aa Calls at Dogdyke 6 43 and Tattershall 6 46 mrn when required to set down
B Station for Market Deeping (3¼ miles)
F Except Saturdays but applies on Sundays
R Restaurant Car King's Cross to Peterborough
S Saturdays only
T Thro Carriage, Skegness to Lincoln
TC Through Carriages
V TC and Buffet Car King's Cross to Cleethorpes arr 8 39 aft (Table 55)
¶ Station closed

25. Moving downstream a little, we see the swing bridge in about 1905, along with the barge facilities. Also evident is a tall white post for the new level crossing gate and an extended locomotive water delivery arm. (Stations UK)

September 1950

Table 72 — WOODHALL JUNCTION, CONINGSBY, and FIRSBY

Miles		Week Days				Suns.		Miles		Week Days		
		a.m T	p.m T	p.m T	p.m S	p.m				a.m T	p.m T	p.m T
	65 Lincoln (Central) ..dep	9 20	..	1 20	6 5	..	1030	..		70 Skegness......dep	8 3	..	12 15	..	4 5	..
—	Woodhall Junction....dep	9 49	..	1 48	6 36	..	1039	11 3	..	—	Firsby.........dep	8 34	..	12 47	..	4 50	..
4½	Coningsby..............	9 56	..	1 55	6 43	..	11 7	..	1111	2½	Little Steeping.....	8 39	..	12 52	..	4 55	..
6¾	Tumby Woodside......	10 1	..	2 0	6 48	..	..	..	..	6¼	Midville..........	8 47	..	1 0	..	5 3	..
9	New Bolingbroke......	10 6	..	2 5	6 53	..	..	..	..	9	Stickney..........	8 52	..	1 5	..	5 8	..
11¼	Stickney..............	1011	..	2 10	6 58	..	..	..	..	11¼	New Bolingbroke....	8 57	..	1 10	..	5 13	..
14	Midville..............	1016	..	2 15	7 3	..	..	..	..	13¼	Tumby Woodside....	9 2	..	1A15	..	5 18	..
18	Little Steeping.......	1024	..	2 23	Aa	..	..	..	..	16	Coningsby.........	9 7	..	1 20	..	5C27	..
20½	Firsby ....arr	1029	..	2 28	7 16	..	..	..	..	20¼	Woodhall Junc.. arr	9 14	..	1 27	..	5 34	..
29¼	70 Skegness..........arr	1055	..	2 57	7 46	..	..	..	..	35¼	65 Lincoln (Cen.) arr	9 55	..	1 54	..	6 3	..

A Stops when required.   Aa Stops when required to set down only.   C Arr. 4 minutes *earlier*.
S Saturdays only.   T Through Train between Lincoln and Skegness.

Table 73 — LOUTH and BARDNEY

Miles		Week Days only					Miles		Week Days only			
		a.m	p.m	p.m					a.m	a.m	p.m	
	Louth ....dep	7 48	..	1240	..	3 57	..	..		65 London (King's C.)..dep	4 0	..	8B30	..	2B18	..
3	Hallington.............	..	..	1246	..	Aa	..	..		65 Lincoln (Central) .. "	9 20	..	1 20	..	6 5	..
4¾	Withcall..............	7 59	..	1251	..	4 8	..	..	—	Bardney ....dep	9 55	..	1 50	..	6 25	..
7¼	Donington-on-Bain......	8 7	..	1 0	..	4 17	..	..	4	Kingthorpe.........	10 2	..	1 57	..	6 32	..
10¼	South Willingham and [Hainton	8 14	..	1 7	..	4 24	..	..	6	Wragby............	10 8	..	2 3	..	6 38	..
12½	East Barkwith ...[Hainton	8 18	..	1 11	..	4 28	..	..	9	East Barkwith ..[Hainton	1013	..	2 8	..	6 43	..
15¼	Wragby..............	8 24	..	1 18	..	4 34	..	..	10¾	South Willingham and	1018	..	2 13	..	6 48	..
17¾	Kingthorpe...........	8 28	..	1 22	..	4 38	..	..	13½	Donington-on-Bain.......	1025	..	2 21	..	6 55	..
21½	Bardney ....arr	8 36	..	1 29	..	4 46	..	..	16½	Withcall...........	1031	..	2 27	..	7 1	..
30¾	65 Lincoln (Central) ..arr	9 3	..	1 54	..	5 39	..	..	18½	Hallington..........	Aa	..	2 31	..	..	..
150¼	65 London (King's C.) "	1 17	..	5B15	..	9D45	..	..	21¼	Louth ....arr	1041	..	2 37	..	7 21	..

Aa Stops when required.   B Via Lincoln.   D Via Lincoln. Arr. 9 35 p.m. on Fridays

26.　A fine postcard view north includes the bay platform for Horncastle branch trains. To reach it, passengers from up trains had to use the crossing in the foreground or the one near the level crossing. (P.Laming coll.)

27.　This is the 1.15pm Boston to Lincoln on 10th June 1947. About two miles before reaching here, it would have passed Coningsby Junction, where the 1912 box had 25 levers, which were in use until 13th July 1964. No. 2172 was a class D2 4-4-0, which was ex-GNR. (W.A.Camwell/SLS)

28.   Seen on the same day is the 1.20pm Lincoln to Skegness, which is hauled by 4-4-0 class D2 no. 2179. In the bay is a train for Horncastle, which will reverse soon after leaving the station. (W.A.Camwell/SLS)

29.   The water column would serve locomotives on both up trains and branch trains. The black structure on the down platform also required water. It was a urinal for gentlemen, made of cast iron panels. (LOSA)

30.   The tank would also supply water to the column seen in picture 25. The large chimney served the boiler for the pump engine, housed at ground level. It was later replaced by an electric pump. Seen in 1953, the wooden canopy supports had been repaired recently. (Stations UK)

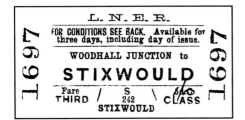

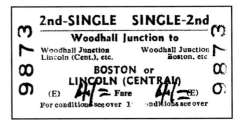

				Week Days only				
Miles		a.m	a.m	a.m		p.m	p.m	p.m
						F	H	P
52	London (King's C.) dep	1 0	4 25	..	10 10	..	1 10	1 10	4 10
—	Woodhall Junction dep	7 15	8 35	..	2 p 0	..	4 45	4 50	7 19	..
1¼	Woodhall Spa	7 21	8 41	..	2 6	..	4 51	4 56	7 26	..
7¼	Horncastle ...... arr	7 37	8 52	..	2 22	..	5 25	7 7	7 37	..

WOODHALL JUNCTION, WOODHALL SPA, and HORNCASTLE

F Except Fridays and Saturdays
H Fridays and Saturdays
P Through Train from Boston, dep. 6 45 p.m. (Table 52)
p p.m.
‡ Via Grantham and Lincoln.

October 1947

31. The 9.00am Lincoln to Skegness was hauled by class B1 4-6-0 no. 61281 on 29th April 1954. The LNER built 409 of these locomotives. The iron convenience became an exhibit at the Museum of Lincolnshire Life, in Lincoln. (R.M.Casserley)

PETERBOROUGH (North), SPALDING, BOSTON, and LINCOLN (via Boston)

Week Days

Miles		a.m M (RC King's Cross to Lincoln (arr 3 15 a.m) via Sleaford (Table 61))		a.m	a.m		a.m		a.m		a.m (RC Skegness to Lincoln)		a.m S		a.m		p.m (RC Skegness to Lincoln)		p.m		p.m F		p.m H
	1 London (King's C dep	11J45	..	1 0	..	..	4 25	..	..	..	..	..	..	..	8R45	..	..	..	..	..	1R10	..	1R10
—	Peterboro' (North) dep	1 35	..	3 0	..	..	6 28	..	..	..	..	..	..	..	1045	..	..	..	..	..	2 51	..	2 51
5¾	Peakirk	..	..	..	..	..	..	..	..	..		..	..	..	1056	..	..	..	..	..	3 2	..	3 5
7	St James Deeping B	..	..	..	..	..	6 42	..	..	..	..	..	..	..	11 0	..	..	..	..	..	3 6	..	3 9
11¼	Littleworth	..	..	..	..	..	6 50	..	..	..	..	..	..	..	11 8	..	..	..	..	..	3 14	..	3 17
16¼	Spalding arr	2 0	..	3 23	..	..	6 59	..	..	..	..	..	..	..	1117	..	..	..	..	..	3 26	..	3 26
	Spalding dep		..	3 33	..	..	7 10	..	..	..		..	..	..	1125	..		..	..	..	3 28	..	3 31
20½	Surfleet		..	..	..	..	7 18	..	..	..		..	..	..	1133	..		..	..	..	3 36	..	3 39
24½	Algarkirk & Sutterton		..	..	..	..	7 25	..	..	..		..	..	..	1140	..		..	..	..	3 43	..	3 46
27	Kirton		..	..	..	..	7 31	..	..	..		..	..	..	1146	..		..	..	..	3 49	..	3 52
31	Boston arr		..	3 52	..	..	7 39	..	..	..		..	..	..	1154	..		..	..	..	3 57	..	4 0
	Boston dep		..	..	6 25	..	..	..	7 54	..		..	1125	..	..	..		..	1 15	..	..	..	..
35¾	Langrick		..	..	..	..	..	..	8 4	..		..	1135	..	..	..		..	1 25	..	..	..	..
42	Dogdyke		..	..	Aa	..	..	..	8 14	..		..	1145	..	..	..		..	1 35	..	..	..	..
43¾	Tattershall		..	..	..	..	..	..	8 17	..		..	1148	..	..	..		..	1 38	..	..	..	..
46¼	Woodhall Junction arr		..	..	6 52	..	..	..	8 24	..		..	1155	..	..	..		..	1 45	..	..	..	..
—	59 Skegness dep		..	..	..	..	..	..	..	..	8 0	..	..	..	..	..	1210	..	..	..	..	..	..
—	59 Firsby		..	..	..	..	..	..	..	..	8 30	..	..	..	..	..	1245	..	..	..	..	..	..
—	Woodhall Junction dep		..	..	..	..	..	..	8 30	..	9 20	..	1157	..	..	..	1 26	..	1 47	..	..	..	..
48¾	Stixwould		..	..	..	..	..	..	..	..	9 25	..	..	..	..	..	..	..	1 52	..	..	..	..
50¾	Southrey		..	..	..	..	..	..	8 37	..	9 30	..	..	..	..	..	..	..	1 57	..	..	..	..
52¾	Bardney arr		..	..	..	..	..	..	8 42	..	9 35	..	12 7	..	..	..	1 37	..	2 2	..	..	..	..
	Bardney dep		..	..	..	..	..	..	8 44	..	9 37	..	12 9	..	..	..	1 38	..	2 4	..	..	..	..
56¾	Five Mile House		..	..	..	..	..	..	..	..	9 45	..	..	..	..	..	..	..	2 12	..	..	..	..
62	Lincoln arr		..	..	..	..	..	..	8 59	..	9 54	..	1228	..	..	..	1 59	..	2 21	..	..	..	..

Week Days—continued / **Sundays**

	p.m F		p.m H		p.m (RC Skegness to Lincoln)		Buffet Car King's Cross to Cleethorpes arr 8 39 p.m. (Table 55)	p.m		p.m (To Horncastle arr. 7 37 p.m. (Table 53))		p.m					Sundays a.m		p.m		Buffet Car King's Cross to Cleethorpes arr. 10 49 p.m. (Table 55)	p.m	
1 London (King's C) dep	..	..	..	..	..	..		4 10	..	..	..	6R5	..	..	..	..	11R20	..	..	..		6 10	..
Peterboro' (North) dep	..	..	..	..		..		5 48	..		..	7 50	..	..	..	..	2 0	..	..	..		7 50	..
Peakirk	..	..	..	..		..		..	..		..	8 1	..	..	..	..	p.m	..	..	..		..	..
St. James Deeping B	..	..	..	..		..		..	..		..	8 5	..	..	..	..	..	..	..	..		..	..
Littleworth	..	..	..	..		..		..	..		..	8 13	..	..	..	..	..	..	..	..		..	..
Spalding arr	..	..	..	..		..		6 12	..		..	8 22	..	..	..	..	2 25	..	..	..		8 14	..
Spalding dep	..	..	..	..		..		6 16	..		..	8 34	..	..	..	..	2 33	..	..	..		8 22	..
Surfleet	..	..	..	..		..		..	..		..	8 42	..	..	..	..	2 41	..	..	..		..	..
Algarkirk & Sutterton	..	..	..	..		..		..	..		..	8 49	..	..	..	..	2 48	..	..	..		..	..
Kirton	..	..	..	..		..		..	..		..	8 55	..	..	..	..	2 54	..	..	..		..	..
Boston arr	..	..	..	..		..		6 37	..		..	9 3	..	..	..	..	3 2	..	..	..		8 43	..
Boston dep	4 10	..	4 15	..		..		..	..	6 45	..	..	..	..	..	..	..	..	3 25	..		..	..
Langrick	4 20	..	4 25	..		..		..	..	6 55	..	..	..	..	..	..	..	..	3 35	..		..	..
Dogdyke	4 30	..	4 35	..		..		..	..	7 5	..	..	..	..	..	..	..	..	3 45	..		..	..
Tattershall	4 33	..	4 38	..		..		..	..	7 8	..	..	..	..	..	..	..	..	3 51	..		..	..
Woodhall Junction arr	4 40	..	4 45	..		..		..	..	7 15	..	..	..	..	..	..	..	..	3 58	..		..	..
59 Skegness dep	..	..	..	..	4 5	..		..	..	..	..	..	..	..	..	..	..	..	..	..		..	..
59 Firsby "	..	..	..	..	4 42	..		..	..	..	..	..	..	..	..	..	..	..	..	..		..	..
Woodhall Junction dep	4 45	..	4 50	..	5 29	..		..	..	..	..	..	..	..	..	..	..	..	4 3	..		..	..
Stixwould	4 50	..	4 55	..	..	..		..	..	..	..	..	..	..	..	..	..	..	4 8	..		..	..
Southrey	4 55	..	5 0	..	..	..		..	..	..	..	..	..	..	..	..	..	..	4 13	..		..	..
Bardney arr	5 0	..	5 5	..	5 40	..		..	..	..	..	..	..	..	..	..	..	..	4 18	..		..	..
Bardney dep	5 4	..	5 9	..	5 42	..		..	..	..	..	..	..	..	..	..	..	..	4 21	..		..	..
Five Mile House	5 12	..	5 17	..	..	..		..	..	..	..	..	..	..	..	..	..	..	4 29	..		..	..
Lincoln arr	5 21	..	5 26	..	5 57	..		..	..	..	..	..	..	..	..	..	..	..	4 39	..		..	..

October 1947

32.   Additional buildings had been erected at the time of the opening of the branch in 1855. The globe is protecting a gas light and is of Sugg's shadow-free style. (LOSA)

33.   Another photograph from the 1960s includes more of the new road bridge for the B1191. The branch dock, on the right, was built with side-loading facilities at the far end. (Colour-Rail.com)

34.   Seen from the disused bay in the late 1960s is a DMU bound for Sheffield. The station became unstaffed on 4th November 1968. (R.S.Carpenter coll.)

35.   Special trains for anglers began with the 7.30am from Sheffield Victoria on 22nd July 1900. They ran on most summer Saturdays and Sundays (wartimes excepted) and in 1964 there was one on the former and three on the latter, all terminating here. The service ended in 1969 and here we see the last return train, together with the gateman's hut. (Stations UK)

36.   Woodhall Junction Box came into use in 1878 and had 50 levers from 1949. It became a points box on 4th October 1970 and closed on 5th April 1971. Passing it on 28th April 1970 is the 08.34 Lincoln to Skegness. The goods-only branch platform is on the right. The yard here was closed on 5th April 1971. (Colour-Rail.com)

37.   We can now enjoy a photograph from 22nd April 2015. The gates here had been worked by gatemen living in the adjacent cottages and working under bell code instructions from the signal box. The Water Rail Way users start here on their 33 mile walk or bicycle ride to Lincoln. The notice boards and windows of the station are replicas of the originals. (Janet Smith)

STIXWOULD

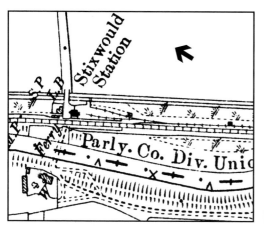

VII. The population was 198 in 1901. The 1904 edition is shown at about 9ins to 1 mile. The two short sidings are included. The station was just over a mile from the village.

STIXWOULD.

Telegraph station at Kirkstead, 2 miles.

In the vicinity is *Tupholme*, at which are the ruins of an abbey built by the Nevilles.

SOUTHREY (Bucknal) station.

BARDNEY. — Here is a cross to the memory of Ethelred of Mercia, who founded the monastery built here in the 7th century, and of which he died abbot.

WASHINGBOROUGH.—In the vicinity are *Canwick*, seat of the Sibthorpe family, and Fiskerton Old Church.

38. The station buildings are single storey and the staff ones are double. An excursion passes through in this northward view, from around 1960. The 1877 signal box had a 20-lever frame and closed on 22nd May 1966. (W.A.Camwell/SLS)

39.   The loading gauge appears in this slightly earlier view, as does the track for the permanent way trolley. This had to be lifted on and off the running lines. There was no goods shed or crane here. The yard was closed on 17th June 1963. (Stations UK)

40.   The crossing served the ferry, which was operated by the signalman and his wife in later years. The wicket gate for passengers can be seen in the previous picture. It could be locked from the box. The house still stands and the signal box was rebuilt close to it. (LOSA)

SOUTHREY

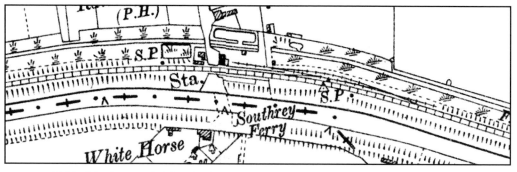

VIII.   The loop and siding is shown on the 1913 survey at about 9ins to 1 mile.

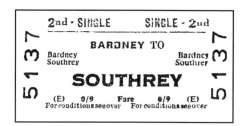

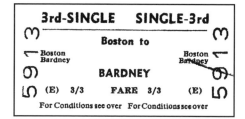

41.   The building positioning was similar to that at Stixwould. This is an early photograph, as it pre-dates the ban on covering sleepers. (P.Laming coll.)

42.   The lane over the crossing led to the ferry which was operated by staff of the nearby White Horse Inn. The signal box was built in 1878 and had 18 levers when closed on 30th June 1963. The goods yard was on the right and closed on 1st October 1955. (LOSA)

43.   A 1969 view includes another wicket gate, to protect passengers from passing trains. The ticket office was open irregularly, as it was staffed by the signalman. The tiny village had around sixty dwellings. (J.A.Evans/HMRS)

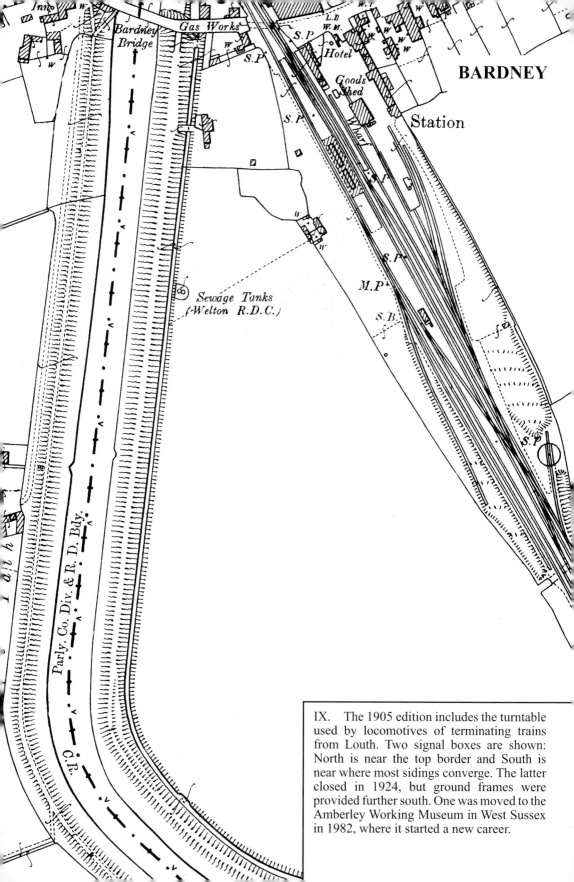

BARDNEY

Station

Bardney
Bridge

Gas Works

Hotel

Goods
Shed

Wharf

Sewage Tanks
(-Welton R.D.C.)

Parly. Co. Div. & R. D. Bdy.

C.R.

S.P.

S.P.

S.P.

S.P.

S.P.

M.P.

S.B.

S.P.

IX. The 1905 edition includes the turntable used by locomotives of terminating trains from Louth. Two signal boxes are shown: North is near the top border and South is near where most sidings converge. The latter closed in 1924, but ground frames were provided further south. One was moved to the Amberley Working Museum in West Sussex in 1982, where it started a new career.

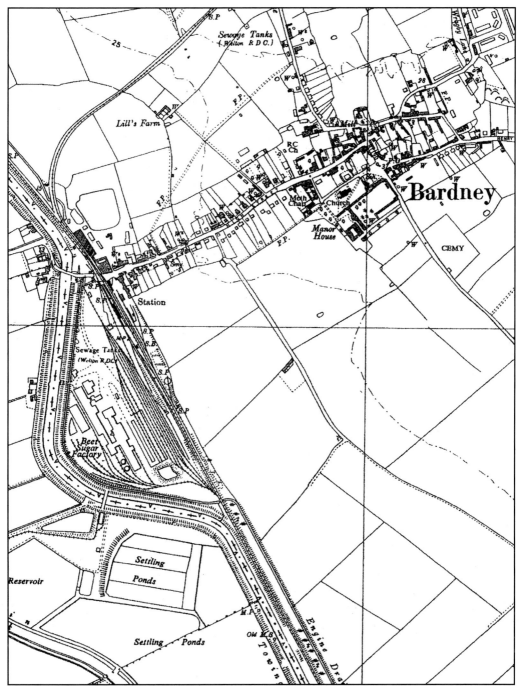

X.   The 1938 revision at 6ins to 1 mile includes the 1927 factory of the Lincolnshire Beet Sugar Company. The coal and most beet arrived over the LNER, but the Nocton Estate (to the west) had 23 miles of 2ft. gauge railways for transport of beet and potatoes. The former was unloaded at its eastern extremity, lower left. The bridge over the river carried a transporter grab and the beet was loaded into standard gauge wagons for conveyance across the yard. They were unloaded along with 30 to 40 others per day, in peak season, until 1951. The 2ft. lines were not shown on the 1948 revision. By 1934, 300 tons of raw sugar were sent by rail to Thames-side refining factories per day, on average. Other material inward by rail annually included 25,000 tons of coal, 9800 tons of limestone and 950 tons of coke. The firm became British Sugar Corporation in 1936 and the last word was dropped in 1982.

44.   The intricate architectural details are worthy of study in this early postcard, franked in 1904. The sleepers are hidden under the ballast, a practice soon to be banned. (P.Laming coll.)

45.   Sent in 1908, this card includes two cloth caps (track workers?), two cap badges (new staff?) and moustaches everywhere. (P.Laming coll.)

46.   The platform face on the right was added shortly after the Louth route opened. This enabled branch trains to use the platform on the left and the island was dedicated to main line services. The track gang trolley could be conveniently moved to and from the track at the level crossing. (Stations UK)

47.   A view from about 1930 features the goods shed, which unusually was listed as devoid of a crane. The white structure is the obligatory loading gauge. (Stations UK)

48.   Moving a little further north, but in 1946, we see a Louth train awaiting a locomotive. The signal on the left allowed up trains to set back to gain access to the branch. Centre is the down main starter and on the right is another down main starter and a branch starter signal on the right. (Stations UK)

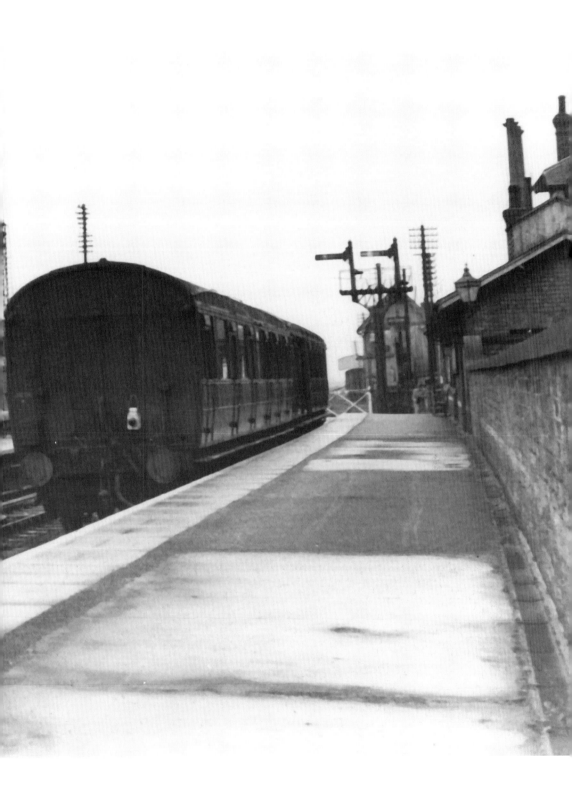

50. Part of the goods yard was recorded on the same day, from a departing train. Shunting is class A5 no. 69804, a type of 4-6-2T introduced in 1911. The coal staithes are on the left. (H.C.Casserley)

49. The barrow crossing was also used by passengers. No weather protection was ever provided for branch passengers. The photograph is from 28th April 1954. (R.M.Casserley)

51.   The station and goods yard are lower right in this aerial view from 1931. The three large roof spans near the former are over the canning works of J.Morrell & Company. Their two sidings were served from the Louth branch. (Lincolnshire Sugar Beet Co. Ltd.)

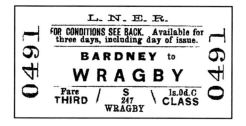

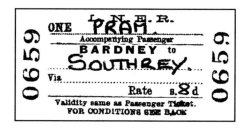

52.   Private owner wagons (left) were common in the 1930s, but diminished during World War II. On the right of this eastward view is the company's Hudswell Clarke 0-6-0ST no. 1604 of 1928. It worked here until 1970. (Lincolnshire Sugar Beet Co. Ltd.)

53.   Sidings were extended in 1943 and the last beet to arrive by barge was in 1950. The last to come by BR was in 1971, the Nocton Estate lines having fallen out of use by 1959. They officially closed in 1969. Ruston diesel no. DS165 was purchased new in 1954 to replace the engine in the previous photograph. The diesel eventually retired to the Lincolnshire Railway Museum and the saddle tank to the Nene Valley Railway. The factory closed in 2001, but liquid sugar was still packaged here until 2011. (Lincolnshire Sugar Beet Co. Ltd.)

54. A DMU is seen arriving from Lincoln on 10th November 1962. The massive ventilators are over the facilities for gentlemen. The goods yard (right) closed on 6th May 1963. (E.Wilmshurst)

55. The Louth branch had mostly been lifted in 1961, but part can be seen on the right. A few years later, a DMU departs for Lincoln. Bardney was unstaffed from 7th October 1969. (R.S.Carpenter coll.)

↓ 56.   This was called North Box until South Box closed on 27th February 1924. Its 45-lever frame was worked until 5th October 1970. To the left of it is the canopy adjacent to one of the two sidings of the canning factory. Most tins arrived from the Metal Box Company in Wisbech, usually daily. Coal was unloaded at the far end of the building and it was also conveyed to the sugar factory until 1982. (J.A.Evans/HMRS)

57. We finish our visit with two photographs from 28th March 1970. The remaining platform had been made less welcoming by the removal of the waiting room. On the left is the 14.00 from Lincoln to Grimsby, while the 15.22 from Firsby departs for Sheffield. (W.A.Camwell/SLS)

58. All notices had been lost, except the sign for gentlemen. The entire station was dismantled and rebuilt on the Nene Valley Railway. The Station Heritage Centre was established here, bearing some of the original signs. It offered refreshments to users of the Water Rail Way, which was established between here and Woodhall Junction for cyclists and walkers to enjoy. (W.A.Camwell/SLS)

FIVE MILE HOUSE

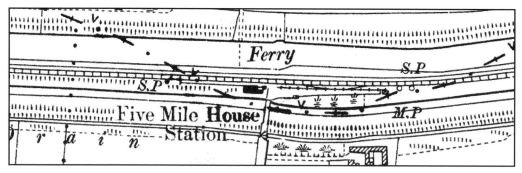

XI.   The station was named after a nearby inn, but all the GNR buildings were destroyed by fire in 1919. Those on the platforms vanished in the same way in 1960. The date is 1913 and the scale is about 9ins to 1 mile.

59.   We look west at ex-GNR somersault signals sometime in 1963. The box replaced the earlier one in 1920 and its 19-lever frame was in use until 31st January 1965. (Stations UK)

60.   The station closed on 1st December 1850, but reopened on 1st September 1865. Closure came for passengers and freight on 15th September 1958, except for anglers trains. These called on summer weekends until September 1964. (D.K.Jones coll.)

WASHINGBOROUGH

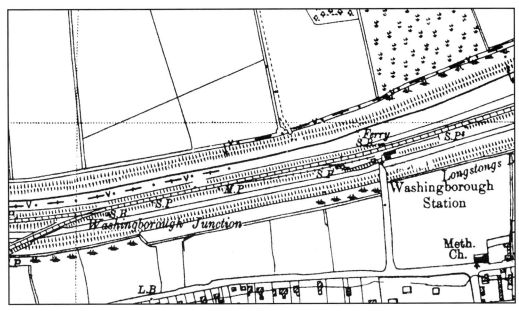

XII. The 1938 edition at 6ins to 1 mile records the limited extent of the goods yard.

61. A riverside postcard includes all the railway buildings, which have now familiar architecture. The residents served numbered 647 in 1901. (P. Laming coll.)

62.   Another postcard and this features the foot crossing for passengers common on this main line. The signal box dated from 1874 and it lasted until 1940. It had only 15 levers. (P.Laming coll.)

63.   Closure to all traffic came on 29th July 1940, the earliest on the route. This is the scene in 1953 looking west. The signals of Washingborough Junction are indistinct in the distance. Its signal box had 16 levers and closed on 3rd March 1965. (Stations UK)

EAST OF LINCOLN

64.   The back cover diagram shows the junctions on the approach to the city from the east. Seen at Pelham Street Junction on 28th July 1979 is the 09.35 Ely to Sheffield DMU. It is just right of centre on the next map. In the background is Sincil Bank Junction Box, a replacement which was opened in 1921. It had 42 levers and was closed on 29th January 1984, the same day as Greetwell Junction Box. Pelham Street on the right had 100 levers and was shut on 19th July 2008. (T.Heavyside)

XIII. The 1898 revision at 2ins to 1 mile. Our route is the centre one on the right border and the River Witham is above it. Shown is a single track link to the line from Sleaford. This became double track later.

65.   A fine view from the 1930s has two LNER class D2 4-4-0s waiting to depart east; they are nos. 4332 and 4329. Adjacent to the water column is a brazier to stop it freezing. Its attendant has a hut and stove nearby. (LOSA)

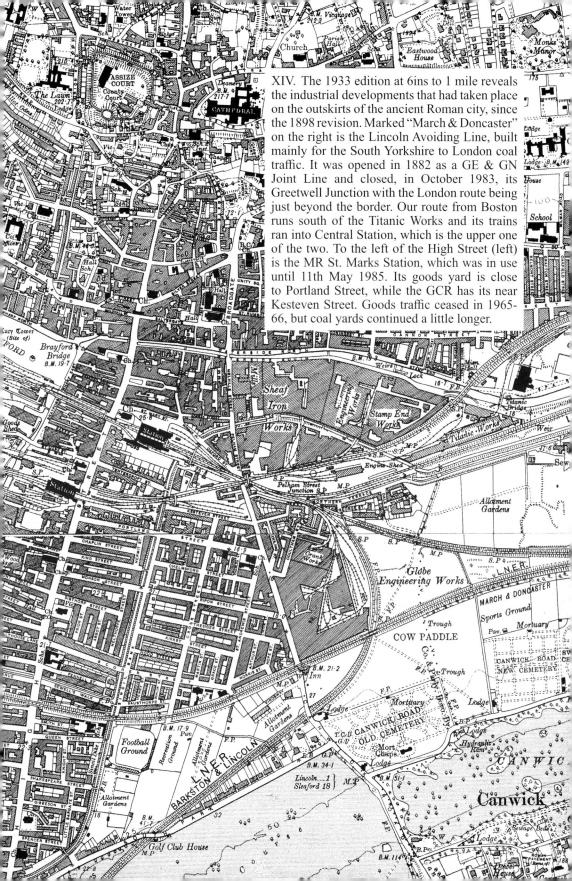

XIV. The 1933 edition at 6ins to 1 mile reveals the industrial developments that had taken place on the outskirts of the ancient Roman city, since the 1898 revision. Marked "March & Doncaster" on the right is the Lincoln Avoiding Line, built mainly for the South Yorkshire to London coal traffic. It was opened in 1882 as a GE & GN Joint Line and closed, in October 1983, its Greetwell Junction with the London route being just beyond the border. Our route from Boston runs south of the Titanic Works and its trains ran into Central Station, which is the upper one of the two. To the left of the High Street (left) is the MR St. Marks Station, which was in use until 11th May 1985. Its goods yard is close to Portland Street, while the GCR has its near Kesteven Street. Goods traffic ceased in 1965-66, but coal yards continued a little longer.

66.　Waiting in the first of four bay platforms for eastbound departures is no. A4009, an LNER (ex GNR) class C12 4-4-2T (it was a rare case of a number being duplicated at amalgamation in 1923 - hence the letter). The date is 10th May 1946. The white windows indicate toilet compartments. (H.C.Casserley)

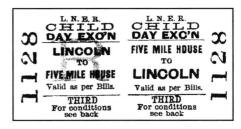

67.   A view west in 1954 shows the footbridge from which the previous two photographs were taken. There were two more through platforms in the early years, but only one of them was needed later. (Stations UK)

68.   It is 11th October 1958 and class B1 4-6-0 no. 61225 is creeping through with a long van train. A Baronial tower with castellations was unusual for a station, but the GNR was generous when it reached here. (J.Chesney)

69.   The north elevation faces St. Mary Street and is seen on 20th September 1975. It remained little altered 40 years later. The term "Central" was dropped when St. Marks was closed in 1985. (D.A.Thompson)

70.   Seen from Platform 3 are both footbridges. The nearest one accommodated a public footpath and provided no access to the platforms. The bay platforms were used by local trains to Boston, Grantham, Grimsby, Skegness and Sleaford. Nos 1 and 2 were no longer in use for passengers. (LOSA)

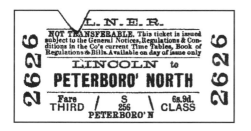

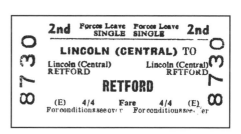

LINCOLN

71.   At the west end of the station, we see High Street Box on 12th April 1986. It had 36 levers and was in use until 19th July 2008. It became a listed building and remains in place. Note the traffic lights needed to create gaps in the dense traffic. The extension at the nearest end is for the separate power-operated levers for the crossing gates. (D.K.Jones coll.)

> **Other Middleton Press albums to feature Lincoln are**
> *Lincoln to Cleethorpes* **and** *Nottingham to Lincoln.*

72.   This eastward panorama is from the station footbridge on 16th July 1992. The public footbridge is partially obscuring the road bridge created in 1958-59 to eliminate the traffic jams caused by Durham Ox crossing at Pelham Street. The inn of that name had been north of it and had to be demolished as a result. (B.W.L.Brooksbank)

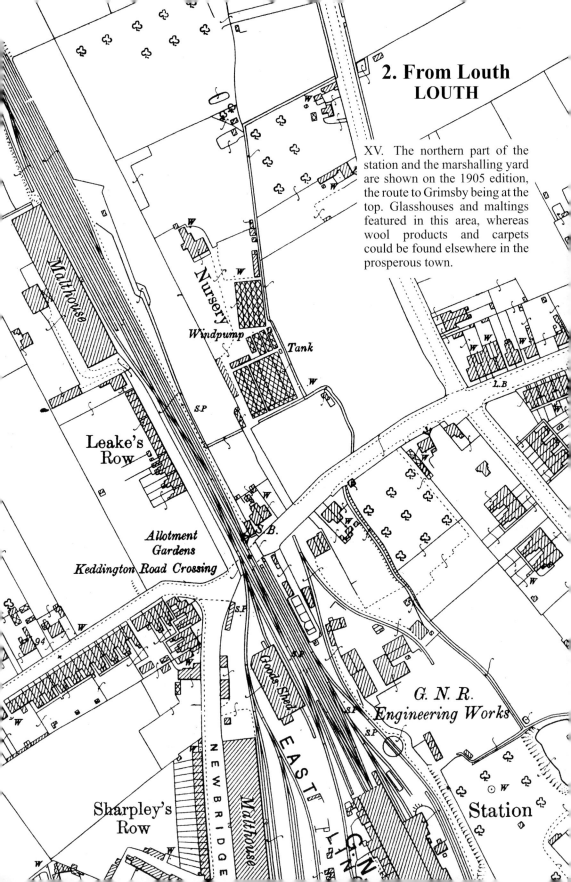

2. From Louth
LOUTH

XV. The northern part of the station and the marshalling yard are shown on the 1905 edition, the route to Grimsby being at the top. Glasshouses and maltings featured in this area, whereas wool products and carpets could be found elsewhere in the prosperous town.

Malthouse

Nursery

Windpump

Tank

S.P.

L.B.

Leake's Row

Allotment Gardens

Keddington Road Crossing

S.P.

S.B.

G. N. R.
Engineering Works

S.P.

S.P.

Goods Shed

Sharpley's Row

Newbridge

Malthouse

EAST L

Station

G.N.

73.   An 1895 postcard reveals the perfect symmetry of the neo-Jacobean style and a horse standing near the substantial porte-cochère. After closure, the building suffered much vandalism, but eventually fell into caring hands, thankfully. North Box was also restored. (P.Laming coll.)

74.   The shunting horse is unclear on the far track. The station had a subway for passengers, a rare feature in Lincolnshire. One noted traveller to Bardney was a stallion, who would call at each station for the benefit of local mares. His groom had an adjacent sleeping compartment in the dedicated van known as a horse box. (P.Laming coll.)

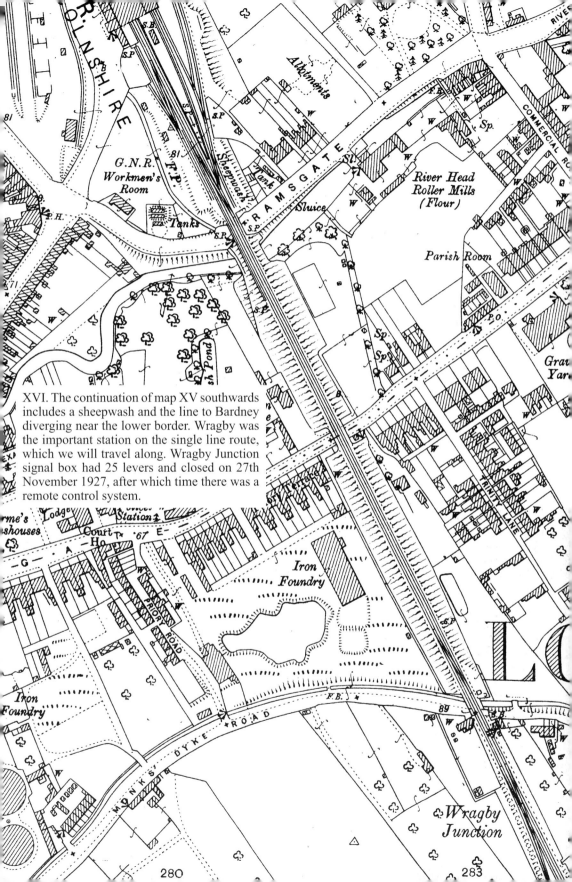

XVI. The continuation of map XV southwards includes a sheepwash and the line to Bardney diverging near the lower border. Wragby was the important station on the single line route, which we will travel along. Wragby Junction signal box had 25 levers and closed on 27th November 1927, after which time there was a remote control system.

75.   We are at the south end of the station on 3rd July 1936 and class D3 4-4-0 no. 4343 waits to leave with the 9.56am to Bardney. The stationmasters office is on the left. Two market days per week had generated much traffic. (H.C.Casserley)

76.   The bay platform was added in 1877 for trains to Mablethorpe. It was also used by those to Bardney, as witnessed on 9th May 1946. Class C12 4-4-2T no. 4548 heads the 3.57pm departure. No. 4525 waits on the right, in the carriage sidings. (H.C.Casserley)

77.	No. 4525 is seen minutes later, from the same platform. The engine became no. 67379 when nationalised in 1948. Coded 40C, the shed had 11 engines in 1950 and closed in 1956. 10 to 12 was the range over the years. (H.C.Casserley)

78.	The water tank and the many ventilators on the engine shed roof are evident. The extension near the lower border was a late addition - a residence for the station master. The date is about 1950. (Milepost 92½)

79.   A northward panorama in 1954 has the dock gates on the left and part of the engine shed on the right. South Box was built in 1887 and had a 43-lever frame. It closed with the line in 1970. (Stations UK)

80.   The RCTS Railtour on 16th May 1954 was hauled by ex-GNR class J6 0-6-0 no. 64199. The white window on the horse box indicates the toilet for the groom; his door was adjacent and the panels were hinged for the benefit of the horse. (J.M.Chesney)

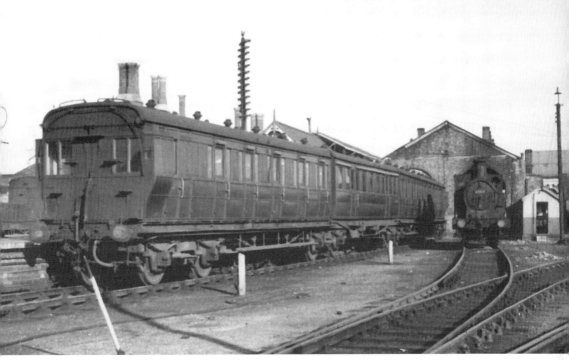

81.   In the bay on 19th September 1954 are four coaches on five bogies, known as an "articulated set". The end windows were used by the driver, when the coach was being propelled by the engine. (F.Hornby)

82.   The splendid roof was lost in around 1960 and this southward view from that era shows vegetable loading equipment. Freight continued to be carried north of here until 1980. (D.K.Jones coll.)

83. The up platform was photographed in 1968, along with evidence of the subway - the windows near the rails. The mail bags were conveyed over the path in the previous picture. (HMRS)

Other views can be found in our
Spalding to Grimsby **album in pictures 79 to 87.**

84. The date is 23rd September 1970 and the end is nigh. This is the rear of the 13.45 Peterborough to Grimsby. This track had been modernised, but the up one still had bullhead rail. (W.A.Camwell/SLS)

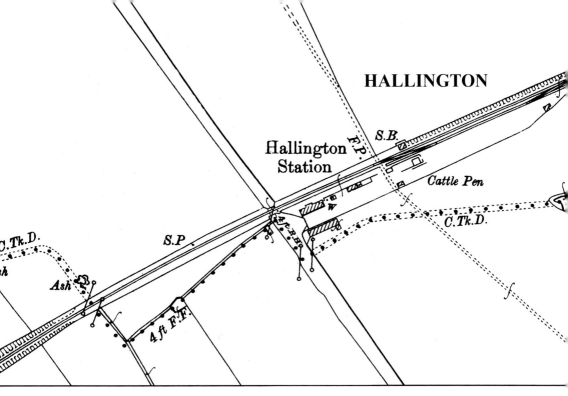

HALLINGTON

XVII.   The village housed 84 souls in 1901 and was almost a mile north of the station, which is seen on the 1905 edition.

85.   The signal box had only 16 levers and remained until line and goods yard closure on 15th September 1956. There was no crane here. (P.Laming coll.)

86. Seen more fully in this 1953 panorama is the parcels shed. Passenger trains ceased on the route on 5th November 1951. (Stations UK)

87. Strawberries and gooseberries bound for Boston were notable items loaded here in the early 1950s. This is the sad scene after closure, but at least the house was not demolished. (W.A.Camwell/SLS)

WITHCALL

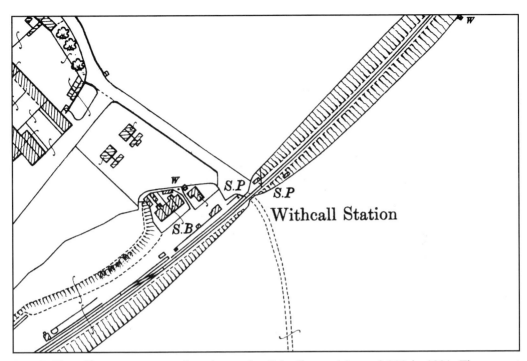

XVIII. The village was scattered to the north of the line and housed 209 in 1901. The nearest dwellings on this 1905 map were for staff.

88.   The 9.55am Bardney to Louth is seen on 10th June 1947, hauled by class C12 4-4-2T no. 7352. It carries NE lettering, not LNER. This was a wartime economy measure. Many boxes of flowers were loaded here, but goods traffic ceased early, as at Hallington. (W.A.Camwell/SLS)

89.   The Wolds can be enjoyed in the distance, but the hills gave rise to substantial gradients on the route; look at the cutting in the previous picture. The station opened after the others on the route, on 1st August 1882, and had smaller buildings. The box opened in 1876 and had just 11 levers; it is seen in 1953. (Stations UK)

90.   After closure, the structure was improved and became a Methodist Chapel. Two tunnels followed: Withcall of 971 yards and High Street of 560 yards. They were around 400ft above sea level and close to the area where the coastal chalk reaches the parallel outcrop of lower greensand. (W.A.Camwell/SLS)

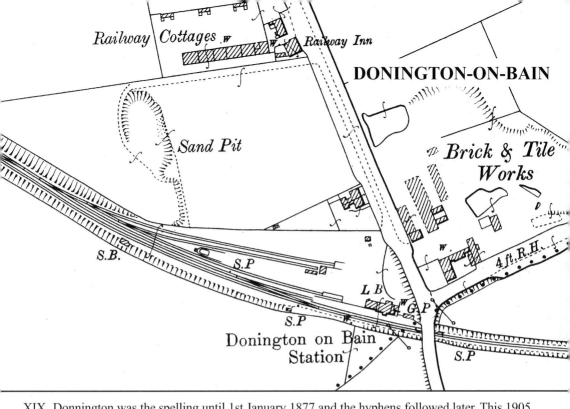

XIX. Donnington was the spelling until 1st January 1877 and the hyphens followed later. This 1905 issue includes the signal box (S.B.), which had served with 25 levers and closed in September 1956.

91.   Seen in 1953, the goods yard seems busy. It was at the eastern end of the branch from September 1956. The route from here to Wragby was closed totally from 1st December 1958. The facility for gentlemen, on the right, is roofless. (Stations UK)

92.   The RCTS railtour in 1954 called to give enthusiasts a rare treat. The last passenger train had left on 4th November 1951, but the building remained standing. The scenic beauty here was great, but little visited. The population was 473 in 1881 and 343 in 1901. (Stations UK)

93.   The scene after closure includes the road bridge, but not for long. The hilly district became a massive bomb store during World War II, serving the numerous airfields on the flatter areas. Thus many extra trains were needed, but one ran free in 1944 and 18 wagons ran away, full of explosives, oscillating between two facing inclined gradients, harmlessly. (W.A.Camwell/SLS)

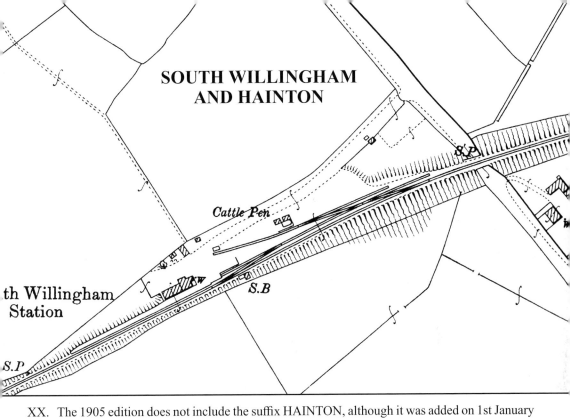

SOUTH WILLINGHAM AND HAINTON

Cattle Pen

*th Willingham
Station*

S.B

S.P

XX.   The 1905 edition does not include the suffix HAINTON, although it was added on 1st January 1877. The number of locals dropped from 283 in 1901 to 209 in 1961.

94.   The 1876 signal box had a 15-lever frame and closed earlier than the others on the route on 6th February 1950. The dock is on the left, as a freight train approaches. The village was ½ mile to the north, but Hainton was a further mile away. (P.Laming coll.)

95.   A 1953 view has oil lamps and name board in place, although the last passenger had gone two years earlier. Strangely, the suffix had become a prefix here, but not on paper. (Stations UK)

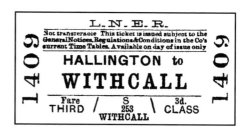

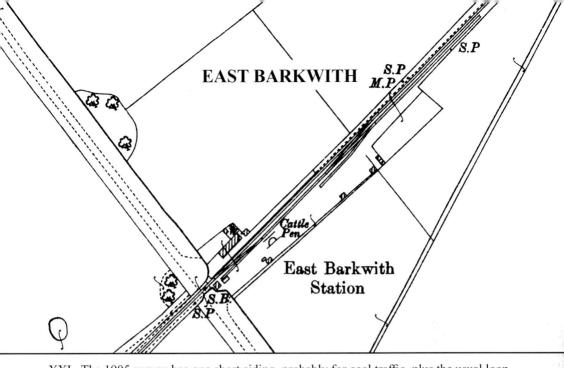

EAST BARKWITH

East Barkwith Station

XXI. The 1905 survey has one short siding, probably for coal traffic, plus the usual loop.

96. Lipton's Tea was promoted despite there being only 307 folk here in 1901 to observe the low enamelled panel. The crossing in the foreground enabled carts to be reversed to the platform for easy transfer of goods. (P.Laming coll.)

97. Here was another 1876 box. It had 16 levers and closed on 1st December 1958, with the route. The compact village was half a mile to the north. (P.Laming coll.)

98. Many chimney pots had been changed, but the building survived to become a private house. On the right is the dock, which once carried a cattle pen. (W.A.Camwell/SLS)

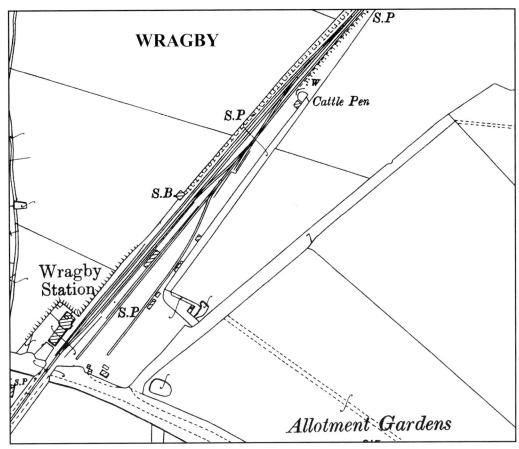

WRAGBY

S.P

S.P

W

Cattle Pen

S.P

S.B

Wragby
Station

S.P

S.P

Allotment Gardens

XXII.   The 1905 edition reveals the largest goods yard on the route. The village contained 494 souls in 1901 and 796 in 1961. It was just beyond the left border.

99.   An early postcard shows little vegetation and a waiting room flanked by two staggered platform faces, on the right. We are down to about 70ft above sea level and there is evidence of local milk production being important. The franking on this postcard was 1907. (P.Laming coll.)

WRAGBY

100. With the main gates open, we gain a glimpse of one of the wicket gates, after a train had just arrived. They were controlled by the gate man, who is seen in the picture after next. (P.Laming coll.)

101. This later view is probably from the 1920s and has uncontrolled vegetation, possibly due to men having been away at war. It brought severe labour shortage. Tapered milk churns have been replaced by modern ones. (LOSA)

102. Another crossing to aid the loading of carts can be seen, as can access to the path to the loop platform. The bricks were buff colour, with red courses for decoration. (P.Laming coll.)

103. The deserted station could be very busy during annual fairs. The one for sheep was on 1st May and for horned cattle the days were 28th and 29th September each year. This floral view is from 1953. (Stations UK)

104. Here we can see the signal box at the far end of the loop points. There had been a private siding listed as Brown's in 1938. (Stations UK)

105. The signal box had 25 levers and closed on 1st February 1960, along with the goods yard and the route. No posters or name boards remain, but one blue board and a green lamp appeared following restoration of the fine building. (W.A.Camwell/SLS)

KINGTHORPE

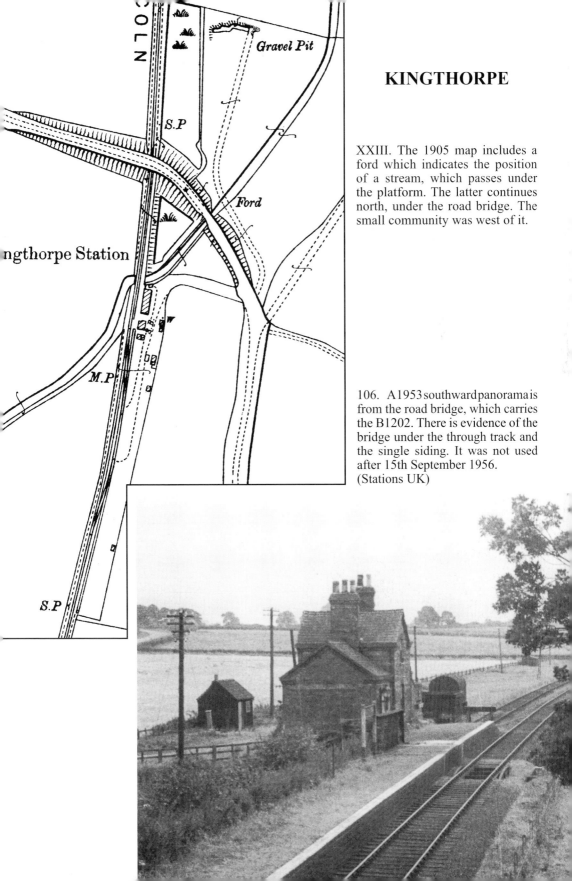

Gravel Pit

S.P

Ford

ngthorpe Station

M.P

S.P

XXIII. The 1905 map includes a ford which indicates the position of a stream, which passes under the platform. The latter continues north, under the road bridge. The small community was west of it.

106. A 1953 southward panorama is from the road bridge, which carries the B1202. There is evidence of the bridge under the through track and the single siding. It was not used after 15th September 1956. (Stations UK)

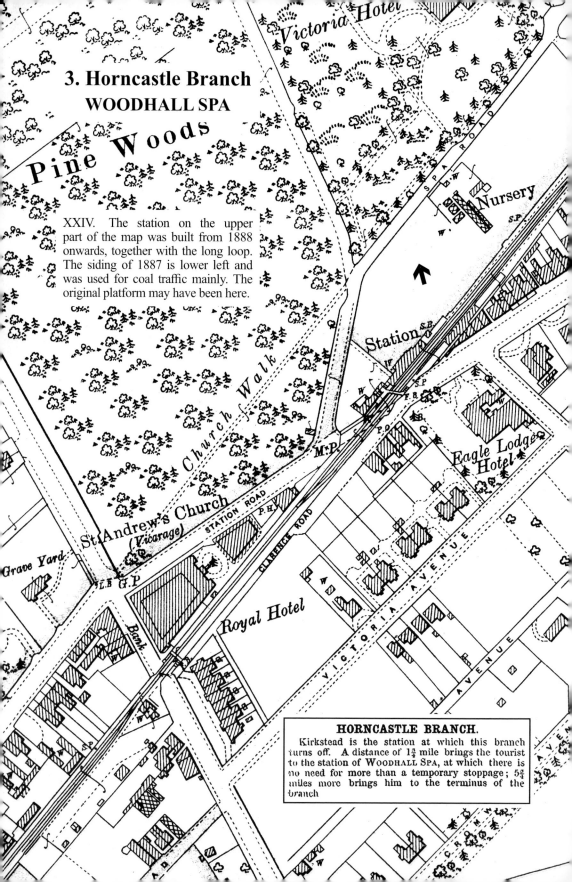

3. Horncastle Branch
WOODHALL SPA

Pine Woods

XXIV. The station on the upper part of the map was built from 1888 onwards, together with the long loop. The siding of 1887 is lower left and was used for coal traffic mainly. The original platform may have been here.

Victoria Hotel

Nursery

Station

Church Walk

St. Andrew's Church (Vicarage)

Grave Yard

Bank

STATION ROAD

Royal Hotel

CLARENCE ROAD

Eagle Lodge Hotel

VICTORIA AVENUE

HORNCASTLE BRANCH.

Kirkstead is the station at which this branch turns off. A distance of 1¾ mile brings the tourist to the station of WOODHALL SPA, at which there is no need for more than a temporary stoppage; 5¾ miles more brings him to the terminus of the branch

107. Tattershall and Stixwould Roads joined at the level crossing near the siding, which is behind the fence on the left. On the right are the footbridge and the massive Royal Hotel.
(P.Laming coll.)

108. Broadway level crossing was at the west end of the station, at the junction with Station Road. Few crossings were at such a small angle to the tracks and few had such long gates.
(P.Laming coll.)

109. A view from the east includes many fine decorative features designed to impress wealthy visitors, notably the chimney stacks. The therapeutic water had been discovered by chance during drilling for coal. The tiny village had grown to 988 by 1901, but visitor numbers could be five times that. (P.Laming coll.)

110. A panorama in the other direction from the footbridge is our final postcard view. The locomotive is no. 292 and is seen in 1909. (P.Laming coll.)

111. The snow is in the winter of 1952-53 and sadly the signalman's stove pipe is in disarray. Sugg's gas lights were chosen, with their Rochester pattern under the roof and the Windsor style on the opposite platform. The train detail is seen better in picture 114.
(P.Ward/SLS)

112. Two photographs from 29th April 1954 are from the opposite side of the same train. Entirely wooden platforms were usually only found on embankments, where weight could be a problem. The timetable extracts show when peak trains ran to and from distant locations. (H.C.Casserley)

113. "Working by train staff" or "One engine in steam" was the rule on the branch until 3rd June 1889, when block signalling came into use. Crossing trains here then became a common practice. The siding was closed on 27th April 1964.
(R.M.Casserley)

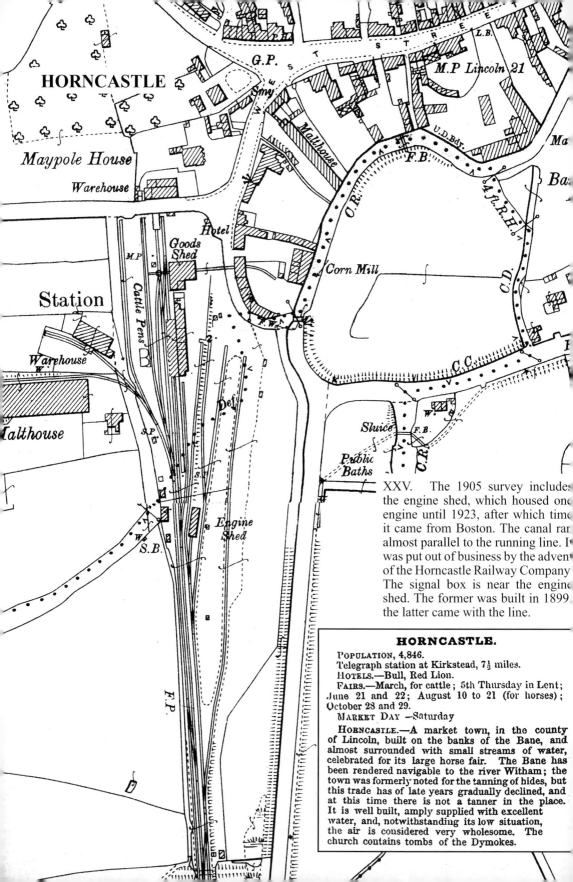

HORNCASTLE

Maypole House

Warehouse

Station

Warehouse

Malthouse

G.P.

M.P Lincoln 21

Malthouse

F.B.

Ba

Ma

O.R.

Hotel

Goods Shed

M.P

Cattle Pens

Corn Mill

C.D.

C.C.

S.P.

Def.

Sluice

F.B.

Public Baths

C.R.

Engine Shed

S.B.

F.P.

XXV.   The 1905 survey include
the engine shed, which housed one
engine until 1923, after which time
it came from Boston. The canal ran
almost parallel to the running line. I
was put out of business by the adven
of the Horncastle Railway Company
The signal box is near the engine
shed. The former was built in 1899
the latter came with the line.

HORNCASTLE.

POPULATION, 4,846.
Telegraph station at Kirkstead, 7½ miles.
HOTELS.—Bull, Red Lion.
FAIRS.—March, for cattle; 5th Thursday in Lent;
June 21 and 22; August 10 to 21 (for horses);
October 28 and 29.
MARKET DAY —Saturday

HORNCASTLE.—A market town, in the county
of Lincoln, built on the banks of the Bane, and
almost surrounded with small streams of water,
celebrated for its large horse fair.   The Bane has
been rendered navigable to the river Witham; the
town was formerly noted for the tanning of hides, but
this trade has of late years gradually declined, and
at this time there is not a tanner in the place.
It is well built, amply supplied with excellent
water, and, notwithstanding its low situation,
the air is considered very wholesome. The
church contains tombs of the Dymokes.

114. This two-car set was dedicated for use on this branch, this being stated above the left buffer. There are two first class compartments above the common bogie and two seconds beyond. A tannery had been demolished to make space for the station, no doubt improving the smell of the small town. (P.Ward/SLS)

115. The branch train is in the bay on 28th April 1954 as a class J6 0-6-0 waits with the 7.57am through train to Boston. This would convey a large crowd of "daily breaders", the term then used before "commuters" were heard of in the UK. Note that GNR somersault signals were in use still. The yard had a 5 ton crane listed by 1938. (H.C.Casserley)

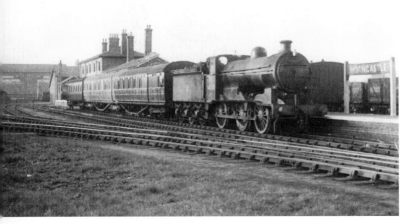

116. Seconds later, we see the same train depart and can now see more details of the locomotive. The rectangular box near the smokebox carried sand to improve adhesion. (R.M.Casserley)

117. About an hour later, we witness class J6 0-6-0 no. 64260 ready to leave with the 8.55am to Woodhall Junction. We have the opportunity to examine the cattle pens, which were regularly very busy. On the left are the malthouse and a lattice steel signal post. (R.M.Casserley)

118. The fine exterior is seen not long before passenger service ceased on 13th September 1954. Freight continued until 5th April 1971 and the building was demolished in January 1985. The branch trackbed was acquired by the county and became the Viking Way for leisure use by walkers. (Colour-Rail.com)

119. The track in the middle had a wagon turntable at its far end and traffic for Harrison's corn mill was hauled from it by the shunting horse, through the goods shed and across the road. The annual Horse Fair could require five special trains in around 1900 and 30 extra men on duty. (LOSA)

120. The platform and the goods shed (left) had been enlarged in 1874, as traffic increased greatly. This 1970s view is of the terminus of a branch, which had produced a good profit in its days of independence. (LOSA)

MP Middleton Press

EVOLVING THE ULTIMATE RAIL ENCYCLOPEDIA

Easebourne Midhurst GU29 9AZ. Tel:01730 813169

www.middletonpress.co.uk   email:info@middletonpress.co.uk

A-978 0 906520   B-978 1 873793   C-978 1 901706   D-978 1 904474
E - 978 1 906008   F - 978 1 908174